MW01135920

JAMES F. QUIGLEY, OP

Living Well

*Homilies/Meditations
on the Virtues*

GREGORIAN & BIBLICAL PRESS

Cover: Serena Aureli

The cover image *The Vision of St. Thomas* by Santi di Tito depicts the saint offering his work to the Lord. In the vision Christ said to Thomas: "You have written well of me, Thomas. What will be your reward?" Thomas answered: "Nil nisi te! Nothing but you!".

© 2012 Gregorian & Biblical Press
Piazza della Pilotta 35, 00187 - Roma
www.gbpress.net - books@biblicum.com

Prima ristampa 2012

ISBN 978-88-7839-**163**-5

TABLE OF CONTENTS

FORWARD

Lent has always been a time for parish renewal programs and retreats. The season obviously lends itself to spirituality. It has been my privilege to offer such weeks of preaching in a variety of parish settings and to groups of young adult Catholics. The focus of these programs was the virtuous life or how to live a better life, how to live well.

The theology behind this collection of homilies/reflections on the virtues comes from St. Thomas Aquinas. His moral vision is based on character development and a theology of grace. His treatment of the virtues centers on the four cardinal virtues of prudence or right judgment, fortitude or courage, temperance or self-control and justice or fairness. He then encircles these with an array of other virtues, e.g. humility, mercy, kindness, patience, etc. Thomas also considers the three theological virtues of faith, hope and charity. All are designed to promote a more human life in the here and now. They are ways of living well, living a better life. The end or goal for such living is ultimate happiness, which for Aquinas, is life with God. These homilies/ reflections then are in a sense a commentary or application of his particular theology.

A preacher is always on the lookout for stories, anecdotes, examples or quotes to clarify the biblical and theological message that is being offered. Those in these homilies/reflections on the virtues have been gathered over many years. Some were told by other preachers or come from long forgotten sources; others are from personal experiences. I am grateful to any and all for their contribution to one preacher's efforts.

I offer this collection as a mark of esteem and respect for my students at the Pontifical North American College. They are now or will in the future be the preachers in the American church. I thank the Rector and faculty of the College for their support and fraternity as well as my Dominican brothers. I honor the memory of Fr. Carl J. Peter and am grateful to the Peter family for their support of the efforts to train good preachers at the North American College.

Fr. James F. Quigley, OP
The Fr. Carl J. Peter Chair of Homiletics
January 28, 2010
The feast of St. Thomas Aquinas

I

HUMAN EXCELLENCE

It seems that no matter where you go in the city of Rome you come across a work done by Michelangelo. The Pieta is in St. Peter's Basilica while the statue of Moses is in the Church of St. Peter in Chains. Whether it is true or not it is alleged that the artist, when asked how he had created something so astonishingly beautiful, said of his work, Moses, that he had merely chipped away at everything not Moses. Moses was in the block of marble, and he, Michelangelo, had simply removed the pieces that did not belong. Another story told of that same statue is that when it was completed Michelangelo then tapped the statue on the knee and said to Moses, "Speak!"

A poet once said: "The saddest words in all the world are what might have been!" It seems to me that the Gospel call to be perfect should not be taken as an indictment or as an occasion to focus on failure. Rather it is a call to fashion and shape the kind of persons we want to be. If you will, we are invited to freely be the artists of our lives. Jesus urges us to discover or realize who we really are, to become the persons we are meant to be. We chip away the extraneous matter that doesn't belong. We do not mourn what might have been. With grace we grow in virtue.

The theologian, Fr. Bernard Haring, has defined virtue as "a form of competence that enables us to grasp the melody of life as a whole and to arrive at that basic option for good that brings all of our thoughts, desires, and actions to maturity." He then adds: "Without virtue, men and women are good for nothing and public dangers." (The Virtues of an Authentic Life)

W.H. Auden once observed: "One of the troubles of our time is that we are all, I think, precocious as personalities and backward as characters." A man or woman of character stands tall and at times stands out. By "character" I mean the accumulated and acquired habits and practices that make a person truly authentic. Behavior flows from the kind of person I am. A good person does good things, and in doing those good things becomes a better person – a virtuous person. It can be second nature to us to be courteous, just, kind, temperate, grateful. Moral competence, competence in being fully human, overcomes viciousness in all its forms – pride, anger, envy, lust, jealousy, deceit.

Moral excellence is not simply about keeping the law or being discreet, nor is it about posing or posturing. A mature adult woman or man plays no games. They take a good look at themselves and see what needs to be changed. They are free enough and grown up enough to face the dark side of their personality, even their sinister self. In a non-compulsive way they examine their conscience and decide on who they want to be and then act. We become what we do.

Walker Percy, the novelist, tells a story in one of his books. A man is sitting on a porch on a hot summer day, rocking back and forth. In front of him on the porch a cat is sleeping in the sun. The man thinks to himself: "that cat is doing exactly what it is supposed to do. It is one hundred percent cat one hundred percent of the time." The man then wonders to himself: "Am I ever one hundred percent of anything? Have I ever been one hundred percent of anything?" The Christian moral life is about growing and becoming fully human, more competent at life and relationships. It is about becoming one hundred percent human. It takes practice and a whole lot of help from others. Most of all, character formation needs the help of God's love or grace. All too often many people of good will become fixated on the negative, on failure or sin, on how they have messed up. A man once told this fear: "My greatest fear is that I will be standing behind Mother Teresa at the final judgment, and I will hear God say to her, 'You know, Mother, you should have tried a little harder and done a little more!'"

The poet says: "The saddest words in all the world are, 'what might have been.'" Women and men, all of us, are called to reach for the good, the true, the beautiful – to seek excellence, to become competent at human living. We are invited to live well, to become the very artists of our lives.

II

LISTENING

A baby's cry, a sick person's moan, a shout of anger, a plea, a curse, a word of love – all of these are sounds and sounds fill the world around us day and night. The question is: do they register? Do we pay attention to them? We probably hear them, at least most of us, on some level of consciousness. But do we listen to them? Hearing, for most of us or many of us, is a pretty automatic act. It involves air waves and receptors attuned to catch sound. Listening is something else. To listen means we intend and attend. To listen means we freely chose to pay attention.

Do husbands listen to their wives and wives listen to their husbands – not just hear but listen? Do parents listen to children? Do children listen to their parents? Not just hear but listen? Do we listen to friends, to each other, to those in need, to the poor, to the sick, to the worried, to the desperate? As religious, Christian, Catholic church people, do we listen? Do we listen to our legitimate teachers and they to us? Do we listen together to the word of the risen Lord, Jesus Christ? To hear is pretty automatic for most of us, but to listen requires intention and attention. We have to freely choose to pay attention.

Do we listen to God? The Bible tells the story of the prophet Elijah who had been summoned by God to meet on the holy mountain. So Elijah travels and stands at the opening of a cave near the summit of the mountain. At first he hears the roar of an earthquake as it cracks rocks and moves slowly up the mountain. God was not in the earthquake. Then Elijah heard the sound of wind as it screams and moans and encircled the mountain, but God, we are told, was not in the wind. Then Elijah heard the crackling of fire as it consumed things in its path but God was not in the fire. And then Elijah heard a very soft gentle breeze rustling the leaves of a small tree. And, we are told, God was in the breeze. Elijah listened and so was able to hear the voice of God in the quiet gentle breeze. (I Kings 19:9-14)

Listening is a virtue, a character trait, a form of respect, the everyday face of charity. Listening is a developed way of relating to other people. A person decides to listen to someone else and to God, decides to deliberately, habitually pay attention to someone, to what they say and to who they are. It is done out of respect for the other. It is, in fact, a choice about being a certain kind of person. Contemporary culture often enough cultivates suspicion. We don't listen. We prejudge. We probe beneath what is said to examine motives and then easily categorize people. We label people as worth paying attention to or not. The Danish theologian Søren Kierkegaard said, "Once you label me, you negate me!" This, of course, is a dehumanizing way to live. It is an absurd way to live. Suspicion and labeling is subversive of community and blocks out true listening. We hear only what we want to hear.

To truly listen can be a way of being a human person. We can cultivate and become a listening person through practice and with grace, but we have to intend and attend. The young French Philosopher Simone Weil writes:

Something in our soul has a far more violent repugnance for true attention than the flesh has for bodily fatigue. This something is much more closely connected with evil than is the flesh. That is why every time that we really concentrate our attention, we destroy the evil in ourselves. If we concentrate with this intention, a quarter of an hour of attention is better than a great many good works. (Waiting for God)

We listen to others when we do pay attention to them and by being respectful of them. We stop centering the whole world and everyone in it on ourselves. We intend and attend to someone else and try to keep silent. We let others finish their message. We don't formulate responses and answers or solutions while the other hasn't even finished their story. We don't simply look for an argument or to dispute or to put down. To listen means that we truly want to understand, because in the final analysis, we are always looking for what is true and real and good.

We listen to God. God speaks to us as a Father in his incarnate son Jesus Christ. And he tells us: "This is my beloved son, listen to him." The Holy Spirit sent by the Son speaks to us but to hear the Spirit of the still living Lord we must pay attention. God's presence to us is often enough a whispered presence, a gentle quiet rustling of the leaves of a tree.

Hearing for most of us is a pretty automatic action. Listening requires intention and attention. We really have to want to listen. Do we do this?

III

GRATITUDE

There is a story told about a little child who woke up in the morning and went out to see his pet turtle. As he looked at the turtle in its bowl, the turtle flipped over and died. The child, of course, was inconsolable. He began to cry and scream and jump up and down. His mother and father came in and tried to calm him. His father picked him up and held him closely, telling him that the first thing that they would do would be to get a matchbox, put the turtle in it and then bring it out to the backyard and bury it. Then after they did that, the father said, they would go to the zoo, which is something the little boy loved to do. The father went on to say that after the zoo they would go to lunch and he could get his favorite macaroni and cheese. In the afternoon they would go to the circus and then after the circus they would go to a store and buy the bike he always wanted. The reaction of the child to all of this was a gradual change. From hysteria he moved to crying and then to whimpering and by the time his father told him about the new bike the little child was smiling and laughing and happy. At that point the turtle once again flipped over and began to move. The father and child seeing this were amazed. The child watched for a moment and then said to his father: "Dad, Dad, let's kill it." That is original sin!

Original sin is not an observable scientific fact unless of course we look in the mirror or drive on a freeway or work for a living or deal with the public or have some responsibility. Adam and Eve had it all – paradise – they even walked with God in the cool of the evening. The great original tragedy was that they were just not satisfied – they wanted more. And because they were unsatisfied, they were ungrateful. The itch to want more, the tendency to be unsatisfied with what we have, is every person's inheritance. We are all, to one degree or another, infected by original ingratitude.

The virtue of gratitude or thankfulness is a disposition of heart, a character trait, a second nature that moves us to see everything that we have as a gift. We did not really do anything to deserve all we have. Gratitude allows us to recognize the one who gives gifts and it urges us to show and express our appreciation.

Have you ever sat down and made a list of all your blessings? Certainly each one of us has played a role in getting some of the things we have or achieving certain things. We have worked and earned and saved and sacrificed. But all of these things were made possible because of gifts, ultimately, from other people and from God – health, intelligence, energy, talent, education, opportunity. You could probably go on and on with this kind of a list. We have received blessings and gifts. It is not just the luck of some cosmic throw of the dice. So, the first element in the virtue of gratitude is to recognize what we have been given. Like all virtues it comes with practice. That won't happen though if we go through life unsatisfied, always looking for more, always asking what have you done for me lately?

The second step in the virtue of thanksgiving is to recognize the donor or the one who gives. The Bible is filled with stories about God's generosity. There is no explaining the why of that generosity. For instance, Jacob deceived his father and defrauded his brother Esau but God blessed him. God blessed David, an adulterer and murderer. God blessed his son Solomon, an idolater and slave master. Matthew's gospel recounts one of Jesus' parables that doesn't make a whole lot of economic sense. A farmer hired people to work in his vineyard. Some began work at sunrise, some mid-morning, others at noon, more in the late afternoon, and a few even just before quitting time. All received the same pay. Needless to say, some workers were unsatisfied. The farmer asked if they thought they were being treated unfairly or were they objecting simply to his generosity? The point of the parable is that God is like that farmer – he is simply a giver and so enormously generous. (Matthew 20:1-16)

Not only could we make a list of all we have received, all of our blessings and gifts but we could also make a list of all those who have been good to us: parents, spouses, children, friends, benefactors and so many others who have gifted us in our lifetime. Some we have never met nor ever known. We shouldn't forget them. We shouldn't take them for granted. We should thank them from the bottom of our hearts.

The virtue of gratitude demands that we express our thanks and then do something in return. The giver or donor does not expect anything in return. He or she has acted out of goodness and pure generosity. He or she has transcended their own self, gone beyond egoism and bestowed a favor on someone else. In doing that, they have become other-centered, benevolent, considerate, self-sacrificing. To them a grateful person opens their heart in thanks and appreciation. This should not be kept secret

19

nor should we assume someone knows that we are thankful. It needs to be said. A grateful person has no difficulty admitting a kind of dependence, a kind the debt of honor to another, and they do their best somehow to return the favor.

Gratitude is not just being polite. Thanks comes from the very core or heart of the person who has received a gift. A thankful person, in fact, walks through life acknowledging all the many gifts they have received. They see life through the prism of the virtue of gratitude. Supposedly there is a school of psychotherapy in Japan that is based on gratitude. There they teach people to see everything as a gift and then, in turn, to deliberately, publicly give thanks. The claim of this school or technique is that the very healing or freeing from neurosis and the traps of self-pity and self-addiction comes when we give thanks.

Being thankful or grateful moves a woman or man to an expansiveness and graciousness. It moves one to imitate the gift giver. To begin to cultivate the virtue of gratitude or grow in thanksgiving it might be a good idea to make a list of all those things that we have received and a list of all those, living or deceased, to whom we owe thanks. Have we been thankful to them? Do they know how much we appreciate them? What precisely can I do for them? Have we forgotten to thank them? Have I thanked God? Am I grateful enough? When we think about it, all of life is a continuous exchange of gifts or should be. Giving thanks is essential if we want to keep the world going.

IV

PATIENCE

We have all met patient people. Perhaps one of the most patient that I have ever met was a young man by the name of Marty. Marty was my student in a college theology course and over the course of his career as a student we became good friends. In high school Marty had been diagnosed with cancer of the hip. It did not stop him from leading as full a life as possible. His cancer would go into remission and then after a time reappear. Marty went on to college but just before his graduation he had to return home for another operation to remove more tumors. Later that same year Marty's leg was amputated. I visited him about a month before he died. He was in great pain at that time and he asked me if I would celebrate his funeral. He knew that the time had come. I remember sitting in his bedroom and the conversation that we had. We spoke a long time about heaven and what heaven would be like. Marty did not complain. He almost never complained. He seemed to me to patiently bear and endure. I asked him if he had become angry with God. His response was that perhaps in the beginning of his cancer he had but after a while had reconciled with God. He said that he really couldn't be angry with God for what was happening to him because so many other people had it much worse than he did. I have met a lot of brave and patient people in my life but I think that Marty was one of the bravest. He absolutely refused to be conquered by fear or hopelessness. He never surrendered his spirit, his zest, his humor, his soul. Marty courageously endured. And that is the virtue of patience. It came from somewhere deep inside him. Marty's patience, his virtue, his endurance were manifestations of God's grace.

The French Philosopher Leon Bloy once said: "There are in the heart of every man and woman places which do not yet exist. Pain must enter in before those places can come to be." Pain, agony, hurt and suffering are facts of life. They are the givens on the human journey east of Eden. It is important that we know how to deal with suffering, not necessarily how to explain it. A father kept grieving and grieving for his lost son. "Why do you keep on weeping" his friends asked, "since it does no good?" The father answered. "That is why I weep, because all my weeping does no good!"

No one can really understand human suffering nor solve the mystery of suffering. Neither can one justify pain. But I am convinced that suffering is never wasted, never forgotten, and I know that if I or we let it, it can teach us. It teaches us the kind of people we are, what is really important, who to turn to for help. It teaches us to see in a new way. Suffering and revelation are connected if we have patience.

Patience is really a form of courage. It is the virtue that enables us to be long-suffering. It teaches us how to be calm in the midst of stress, trials, and provocations. Patience is endurance. It is not stoic resignation. Rather it is a free, active, deliberate choosing to endure an unavoidable affliction and not be conquered by it. Patience enables us to bear any burden that must or should be carried without complaint or undue anxiety. That is not to say that a person is insensitive to their own or someone else's pain. The patient woman or man clearly recognizes the burdens of life but refuses to be discouraged or shaken by them or to lose composure. Patience is an interior quality of a person that produces calm in the face of chaos, peace in the face of pain, strength at a time of disaster.

Life offers a person many choices. We are responsible for those choices. However, there are things in life over which we have little or no control. There are things that we must accept and then endure. To understand this, not to panic but to conform to the reality of our existence and to suffer it, is to be patient. To continuously rebel against our lot in life is to live in conflict and that gets us nowhere. Patience is the other side of the virtue of acceptance. The virtue of patience enables us to hang in there with calm. It does not eliminate burdens or the crosses and trials of life, but it makes them at least bearable and gives us strength and wisdom. The proper object of patience is some kind of burden that we can't escape. Freely, deliberately, empowered by grace, we endure without complaint. We develop this kind of patience by learning and practicing endurance in the face of lots of little lesser trials or annoyances. We put up with rude behavior, shabby treatment, cutting remarks, inconsiderate words and actions, being ignored or taken for granted, being imposed upon. We put up with obnoxious people or people who, for whatever temperamental reason, strike us the wrong way. We patiently endure.

We practice the virtue of patience or long-suffering and we do it as often as we can. Then gradually we become patient people. Since all the virtues are connected and grow together, like the fingers on a hand, patient people become loving, accepting, courageous women and men. The patient person refuses to pick fights or get back; they refuse to give in to a short fuse, to insult or pout or blow up or lose it. By practicing the virtue of patience, a person becomes even tempered balanced, steady, easy-going, peaceful.

We endure patiently because, when all is said and done, we live with the hope of a world without end, a world beyond sorrow and affliction. This too shall pass! We believe and trust the Lord when He promises: "I have come that you might have life, life in abundance." We wait and can get through anything because we really believe that: "Eye has not seen nor ear heard nor has it even entered into the mind of a man or woman what lies in store for those who love God!" (I Corinthians 2:6)

V

HONESTY

Over the years I have presided at a good number of weddings. Many things stand out during these liturgies – the evident faith, the hope, the love of the couple and of their families and friends. But also what is deeply moving is the obvious honesty of the two young people marrying each other. In marriage they give their word. They promise. They speak an oath. The word they speak is their truth. I promise to be true to you always until death in word and action. I promise! You have my word! I vow! I do!

Honesty is a virtue whereby in speech and action a person is real. What you see is what you get. A person both in life and speech presents who they are to the world and presents everything else in the same way.

I'm not sure honesty or truthfulness is as valued today as it should be. So we can read quips like:

– lie about others as you would like them to lie about you.

– many people don't lie; they merely present the truth in such a way that no one recognizes it.

– those who are honest as the day is long have to be watched after the sun goes down.

– a commentary on our times is that the noun honesty is often preceded by the adjective "old fashion."

– the honesty of some politicians has never been questioned. In fact, it has never been mentioned.

Not long ago I had a discussion with my college theology class about the advisability of establishing an honor code at the school. In effect that meant everyone would promise, give their word, vow, never to cheat and also to report anyone they caught cheating. Almost all students balked at reporting or telling on someone else. Somehow it was thought to be "un-American." To be a squealer, a tattletale, to "rat" on someone was simply inconceivable. Some students said that they would not cheat unless absolutely necessary. They considered themselves to be honest people. A few were honest about cheating and said it had to be done at times. You had to do it because of competition, the need to get ahead, and it was no big deal really.

Honesty suggests a kind of transparency or openness. An honest woman or man does not fool anyone nor do they fool themselves. They habitually reject any form of deception or dissembling. Because of this, they become credible and trustworthy to others. Truthfulness suffuses their personality and they can be counted on, they can be believed. But more than that, an honest woman or man possesses integrity and self-worth. They are truly sincere people.

In the gospel of John, we read that Jesus speaks strongly to his opposition: "You belong to your father, the devil ... he does not stand in the truth, because there is no truth in him. When he tells a lie, he speaks in character, because he is a liar, and the father of lies!" (John 8: 44, 45) Untruth, to one degree or another, is evil and wrong. It does no good and can really be harmful.

I remember many years ago as a child waking up and hearing my mother and father talking in the kitchen.

My father was a professional fire fighter and at a fire he had found a wallet with lots of money in it and no identification. Money was scarce in those days. My father told my mother he turned the wallet in, all of it. When other friends found out about it, they laughed. They thought my father was silly and just not too smart. And that's what troubled my father – some, even friends, did not understand or appreciate or like his honesty. My father that night did not intend to teach me a lesson about honesty. However, he did and I have never forgotten it.

Jesus tells us: "...everyone who belongs to the truth listens to my voice." He also tells us: "I am the way, the truth, and the life." (John 14:5) Honesty or truthfulness is a virtue. With it I present myself to others and to all the world. I live in the light and not in darkness. I speak the truth and I do the truth. I imitate Christ the Word of God, God's truth, and that truth makes me free. Flannery O'Connor said that it also makes you odd. But so what!

VI

GENEROSITY

A virtue is a kind of automatic response to a situation. It is not instinctual but rather a cultivated habit, learned behavior, a disposition to act in a certain way. The virtue of generosity or unselfishness inclines a person to always think of others first. Generosity is related to such words as "gender," "generate," "generation," and derives from a Latin word, "genus" meaning a "kind" or "class" of something. We are all of one kind. Generosity in effect means giving to others to whom we are related or connected – other human persons. We are all in a very real way "kinfolk" and so we behave unselfishly.

There is a story told about a child in Alabama. The day was cold and the child stood on a grating in front of a store trying to keep warm. He was poor and not adequately dressed to keep out the cold. A woman passed the child and then went into the store. When she came out, she had bought the child a sweater and shoes and gave them to him. The child, of course, was so excited that he jumped up and smiled and then began to run home. He stopped, though, and then came back to the woman and asked her: "Are you God's wife?" The woman smiled and said: "No, I am just one of his children." The child smiled back and said to her: "I knew we were related."

Elements in our culture fixate on the "self." We hear such expressions as: "Be good to yourself, "self-made men or women," "low self-esteem," "poor self-image." Now there is no doubt that such expressions can have validity, but our culture or at least some of it promotes addiction to self, selfishness, self-centeredness and just plain stinginess.

The human self, the human person is created to know and to love, to relate, to be conscious and to be free. The self in varying degrees is a subject free to act and decide and so can be responsible for the person they are. An unselfish woman or man fashions their way of being in the world. It is the way they choose to be a person, to be responsible for themselves. The generous are those who freely go outside of the self to promote the human good of another. There is irony here which Jesus often noted. He said: "Unless a grain of wheat fall and die, it cannot produce fruit, but if it does, it produces a great abundance". (John 12: 24) Again he said: "He who finds life will lose it, whoever loses his life for my sake will find it." (Mark 8:35) Jesus teaches that human authenticity can only be found in escaping from the prison of self. To the extent that we wrap ourselves up in self-interest to that extent we diminish ourselves. Generosity describes a giving person who is kind-hearted, charitable, unsparing, munificent. A woman or man is affectively touched or moved to give out of solidarity with others. They are neither miserly nor patronizing. They simply recognize their interdependence with others and everyone's dependence on God. They think of others first. If you will, it is their way of paying rent for their space on the planet.

Jesus, of course, is the supreme model of generosity. By our unselfishness we imitate his extraordinary giving. Saint Paul tells us: "Do nothing out of selfishness... rather humbly regard others as more important than yourselves ... each looking out for the other person's interest. Christ even though he was in the form of God ... emptied himself, taking the form of a slave, becoming obedient to death, even death on a cross!" (Philippians 2:3, 4, 7, 8)

A mother told this story about her son. One Christmas she told her children not to give her or her husband presents for the holiday but rather to give money to poor families in the area. She tells us that her son, Chris, was a hockey player at college and could only stay home on Christmas day since he had to leave for a hockey tournament. As he got in the car to leave, his mother came out to say good-bye to him. Chris, the son, said to his mom: "Here, take this for the poor families" and he put money in her hand and then left. The mother looked and saw that he had given her fifty dollars. He had saved that money for a long time. She said she ran after him down the driveway before he drove away and waved him down. She got into the car and sat next to him and held his hand for a little while. At that moment she tells us her son Chris was no longer twenty years old but five years old. She remembered when someone had stolen his new hockey stick. At that time he had said: "Mom, I guess someone else must have needed it more than me." The mother got out of the car and said to her son: "Honey, I love you, and God bless you for this gift." Then she went on to say: "I'll never forget that moment. In that moment I saw Christ in my son." Do we dare to be Christ?

VII

COURTESY

Self-improvement has become something of an industry today. There are all kinds of books and sometimes just plain gimmicks that address physical, social, intellectual, psychological or financial improvement. Some of this material addresses spiritual improvement and that seems to be on the minds of a lot of people. A great deal of money and effort have gone into supporting the efforts to become better people. One sure way to improve yourself, however, and it won't cost money, and it can be done all the time and almost everywhere you go and it really does make you better, is to be polite or to be courteous.

The dictionary defines courtesy as excellence of manners or social conduct; polite behavior, respectful or considerate actions and expressions. The word courtesy suggests other words: graciousness, civility, consideration, thoughtfulness, politeness. Courtesy traces its roots back to the life of royal courts or courtly behavior. The English word, "polite" which means something similar to courtesy, comes from the Greek word "polis," which means "city," and signifies speech and behavior which is courteous or mannerly. We get other words from polis – political, police, policy. Civility derives from the Latin word, "civis" which means "city." So by extension it can be concluded that a city is a place where civil people gather. From civis we get such words as civilian and civilization. Civilization rests on mutual civility, politeness, graciousness, and courtesy.

Not so long ago a news item told a story of road rage. A pickup truck on Interstate 95 evidently was traveling too slowly for the Lincoln Continental behind it. When the truck exited, the Lincoln followed, pulled alongside, and the driver fired a gun at the man driving the truck. Road rage mirrors any number of other rages on streets, in the office, in stores or schools and even in homes. More and more we read about or experience rude and outrageous behavior and speech. People seem to find it just very difficult to be polite or civil to one another.

Politeness, of course, is the result of good upbringing. Children are taught and trained to behave, to act graciously. Adults, on the other hand, choose patterns and ways of acting and these acts produce, if done often enough, a kind of spontaneous way of approaching and addressing another person. Adults presumably are responsible for what they do and who they are. The virtue of courtesy makes one thoughtful, considerate, gracious in speech and in action. It is not about grand things. Rather courtesy is the everyday response to everyone we meet. We communicate and interact with friends or strangers in hundreds of little ways all the time. We can do this with respect and reverence for another or with a kind of savageness. St. Paul urges us to, "Anticipate one another in showing honor and aspire to live a tranquil life" (Romans 12:9, 10) and St. Peter urges something similar: "All of you... be sympathetic to one another. Do not return evil for evil or insult for insult – return a blessing." (I Peter 3:9)

A courteous or polite woman or man decidedly wants to make life easier for someone else, to lighten their burden. In word and deed the worth and dignity of another is thoughtfully regarded and announced and appreciated. Each person is honored because they are unique. They are not diminished or disposed of or despised. Everyone has feelings and wants to be treated with respect – not ignored or worse. That means that courtesy requires sensitivity and time. We have to try and see others the way Christ sees them. We have to see grace in them. Life for most of us is pretty fast paced, and many human encounters during a day are either onetime events or anonymous. Other relationships are on a steady daily basis – people we work with or live with or our own families. The danger for the first kind is that we simply fail to see another human being. They are invisible to us or are seen solely in terms of their usefulness. They don't really matter to us. On the other hand we can tend to take others, those close to us, for granted and assume they know our respect. Little by little, without courtesy, life becomes vulgar and hard and rude and violent.

The virtue of politeness is not mere etiquette or good form. It has to be sincere. Courtesy gives style to our human interactions. It humanizes us and the other person precisely because of the high esteem we have for other people. Like all the virtues, courtesy takes practice. At times it can be pretty easy. However, with some people it takes a great effort. If we are polite enough it gets easier. Key to this virtue is our attitude or perception of someone else. Can I revere and respect another person? Can I revere and respect another, no matter how off-putting they may be? Courtesies, polite acts and words make life more sacred for everyone. They also set the stage for more virtuous behavior which is needed to keep the human community going.

VIII

ACCEPTANCE

"You just have to resign yourself to the fact...!"
"I turned in my resignation – I resigned...!" The word, "resignation" suggests in the first case a kind of passive suffering and in the second case it means that one quits. Older spiritual writers spoke of the virtue of resignation but
that word today can connote weakness, compliance, pas-
sivity, submission or quitting. Perhaps it would be better to
speak of the virtue of acceptance. "Acceptance," suggests
a free and decided act or pattern of behavior in the face
of the inevitable.

There is a scene in one of Tennessee William's
plays. An older woman, slightly confused, sits at a table in
a garden working on a jigsaw puzzle. Most of it is done,
but as she tries to put one of the few remaining pieces into
its proper spot it won't fit. She becomes increasingly agitat-
ed and upset. At that point her daughter comes from the
kitchen into the garden, takes the piece from her mother's
hand and places it in the puzzle, exactly where it belongs.
With that her mother smiles and relaxes. Whether we ad-
mit it or not, when we are really honest with ourselves,
most of us would like to be in control. We want things
to be the way we want them to be. We want things to fit,
to make sense, to be understandable. We don't like chaos,

trauma, confusion. We don't like the feeling of being lost or at the mercy of people or events or forces over which we have no control. Of course, you don't have to be too old to know that life can take unexpected turns. Life can throw us a curve ball. Things can happen to us or to those we love over which we simply have no control. It may seem that we have nothing to say about the matter. Or do we?

A fairly young woman, Anne, with children, suddenly loses her husband. She is left a widow to support her family. Once her children are grown, she continues to live by herself always in love with her deceased husband. Her life is bittersweet in old age – not unhappy, but she is alone and without the love of her life.

Mark and Teresa had a great life, a great family and great prospects for a long and happy life. Then one day Jack, their son, was hit by a car while riding his bike. Jack almost died but survived. He is now a young man confined to a wheelchair and breathes with the help of a respirator. The accident happened some nine years ago. Mark and Teresa have gone through a number of stages and have come to terms with Jack's condition and his future. They live with it all. But there is always a deep regret and sorrow that it has turned out this way.

Another case: Connor and Meg are both in college now. Their mother works hard and gives them a good home. Their father abandoned them, took off and left them with nothing. When it happened, they were devastated, hurt, and angry. They were also afraid and for some reason felt guilty. They now have adjusted and, in fact, at some point in the future might even be willing to meet with their father again. However, they need more time before they do that. They live with a dull pain and regret for not having a "normal" family!

What to do in the face of sickness, disability, death, loss, setback, disappointment, sorrow? What to do in the face of the crosses life can impose? Rebel? Complain? Despair? Be angry? Become embittered? Or accept?

The virtue of acceptance is the habit or disposition to freely accept reality. The accepting woman or man freely chooses to recognize the situation as it is and freely chooses to accommodate to what is, to reality — freely chooses to live with it courageously and peacefully. The virtue of acceptance does not permit escape into fantasy or denial. It does not allow surrender. It runs from defeatism or depression. It rejects the thinking that says you are a victim.

Life can be very difficult. There is no doubt about it. We may daydream about what might have been, but that only brings frustration. Acceptance of life's conditions, its limits, its burdens, its joys and its sorrows is simply surrendering in faith to God's providence. St. Thomas Aquinas tells us that providence is God's individual plan for each one of us as we move toward communion with God. Acceptance empowers us to receive what God in one way or another wills for us or allows us to bear, even if it be pain, hurt, abandonment, loneliness, fear. We don't do this in a morbid way nor with placid indifference. We accept with bravery and trust and in powerlessness offer our cross to God, convinced that God is a loving Father. Certainly, we can feel at times discouraged, overwhelmed, melancholy or even angry. It is then that by a sheer act of the will, moved by grace, we pull, from the deepest part of ourselves, the virtue of acceptance.

Acceptance is not giving up or rolling over. It is deliberately taking reality to ourselves in responsible freedom. It is an act of confidence in the "One" behind and in that realty. It is essentially an act of communion with the mystery of the One and Triune God who is Father, Son, and Holy Spirit.

Reinhold Niebuhr, the American Protestant theologian, caught the essence of the virtue of acceptance in his famous "Serenity Prayer":

> God grant me
> Serenity to accept the things I cannot change
> Courage to change the things I can, and
> Wisdom to know the difference –
> Living one day at a time;
> Enjoying one moment at a time;
> Accepting hardships
> As the pathway to peace;
> Taking as He did this simple world
> As it is, not as I would have it
> Trusting that He will make all things
> Right if I surrender to his will;
> That I may be reasonably happy in this life
> And supremely happy with Him forever in the next.
> Amen.

IX

FAITH

Elie Wiesel, the Nobel laureate, tells a story of a "beadle." A beadle was an official of the Jewish synagogue. In the Warsaw ghetto each day the beadle would walk down the street, go into the synagogue, up into the pulpit and announce: "Master of the universe, we are here." And then the destruction of the Warsaw ghetto began under Hitler. Still, each day the beadle would walk down the street, into the synagogue, up into the pulpit and announce: "Master of the universe, as you can see, we are still here." Then, as history records, the ghetto was utterly destroyed. The beadle was the last person alive in that ghetto. Still, he walked down the street, into the synagogue, up into the pulpit and announced: "Master of the universe, I am still here." But he then added: "But where are you?" (Night)

Speaking about the Holocaust Wiesel stated: "One does not understand Auschwitz with God; one does not understand Auschwitz without God." Events, and certainly tragedy and human suffering, but sometimes just life in general, can test our faith in God. Life and human suffering, of course, can also deepen our faith in God. The Second Vatican Council has defined faith as that by which a person freely and totally commits himself or herself to God.

The gospel of Matthew tells us the story of Jesus coming to the disciples walking on water. The disciples were in a boat and were going ahead of Jesus to the other side of the lake. During the evening a storm arose. The boat was tossed by waves and strong winds. Matthew recounts that during the fourth watch of the night Jesus came toward the disciples, walking on the water. The disciples were terrified and thought it was a ghost. Jesus spoke to them and said, "Take courage it is I; do not be afraid." Peter then responded: "Lord, if it is you, command me to come to you on the water." Jesus responded, "Come." And so Peter left the boat and began to walk on the water toward Jesus. Realizing, however, what was happening and feeling the wind he became frightened. With that he began to sink and cried out, "Lord, save me." Immediately Jesus stretched out his hand and caught him and said, "Oh, you of little faith, why did you doubt?" He then calmed the wind and the sea and all in the boat honored him. (Matthew 14:22-33) Jesus worked a miracle and calmed the sea and wind. He also calmed the disciples. The miracle was an example of power as well a sign of salvation and rescue. Jesus gently criticized the disciples for not trusting, for not believing that he would take care of them in their need no matter what. And at the same time he understood their temptation to discouragement and hopelessness and fear.

Matthew's gospel is not suggesting that belief or trust in Jesus will allow us to sail around every storm. Rather the promise of Jesus is to bring us through everything in one piece. Sometimes pains, worries, crisis, fear can drive us crazy, and the miracle is to just survive and get through it. Faith is not a guarantee that we will not go under or be swamped. It is a promise that even if we nearly drown, Jesus will be with us. Life can seem very unfair at times for all; it can seem unfair always for some. However, faith, the gift and virtue, will allow us, in the midst of storms, to hear and catch the words of Jesus – "Be quiet! Be still! Be calm! I am here!"

Human faith or trust is a personal option. We decide to trust someone, to put our faith in someone. What moves us to do that is our relationship with them. Another person, known and respected as credible, motivates us to accept what they say or do as true. Even when we have no compelling evidence, we believe them. We do that because of our confidence in their believability. The psychology of the act of faith moves back and forth: from goodness to truth, from appreciation and respect for someone to confidence in them to ascent to what they affirm. I believe you and so believe what you say.

I don't know to what extent we live in a culture of suspicion. It does seem that more often than not we are hesitant to believe. People and institutions have disillusioned us and it is just harder to trust. We are less inclined to give others the benefit of the doubt. And yet we simply can't live decent human lives in an atmosphere of suspicion. We need the virtue of faith. We need to recapture the habit of belief.

Religious faith is in some ways like human faith. Yet to believe in God, Father, Son, and Holy Spirit, we need that very God's help and grace. Incredible as it may seem, God wants to love and be loved. Faith in the God who reveals or communicates self to us in and through the risen Lord, Jesus Christ and his Spirit makes that relationship happen. We believe that the Trinitarian God abides in us. St. Paul tells us: "It is no longer I who live, but it is Christ who lives in me!" (Galatians 2:20) John's gospel tells us: "I do not pray for these only, but also for those who believe in me through their word, that they may all be one; even as you, Father, are in me and I in you, that they also may be in us ..." (John 17:20, 21)

The virtue of religious faith enables us to live in intimate friendship with God. We believe and that shapes our whole vision of reality. The world and history and life have meaning and purpose. We believe in the possibility of goodness and worth, our own as well as others. We believe in the promise of fullness of life and salvation. Evil and suffering can never be the final word. Our faith in the Lord, our trust in God, Father, Son, and Holy Spirit pushes us to hope, to dream, to be convinced that God is with us, loving and caring and saving and raising us up. St. Paul says: "For by grace you have been saved through faith, and this is not your own doing; it is the gift of God." (Ephesians 2:8)

There is a scene in Mark's gospel that perhaps captures best the human journey of the virtue of faith. A father asks Jesus to free his son from a violent evil spirit. He says: "... if you can do anything, have pity on us and help us. And Jesus said to him, 'if you can? All things are possible to him who believes.' Immediately, the father of the child cried out and said, 'I believe; help my unbelief.'" Perhaps that is a prayer we can all say and say it often.

X

TRUST

Friars often tell stories about the lives of their own brothers. One such story that has been passed around is about Fr. Bert. Bert was a great professor of philosophy, a scholar and wonderful teacher. Fairly early in his career he contracted diabetes. That disease progressed to such an extent that eventually both of Fr. Bert's legs were amputated. But still he continued to teach and serve the brethren. At one point he was asked to serve as a pastor and superior. He began his role as superior by making some changes to the schedule. In fact, he changed lots of things. As you can guess some changes did not always sit well with everyone. One parishioner was so upset by these changes that he asked to meet with Fr. Bert. He came into the office where Bert was sitting behind his desk. He let go a barrage of criticism for the changes in schedule and the way it was done. He offered a number of arguments to reverse the decision. Bert sat there and listened. When the man was finished Bert, sitting in a wheelchair, pushed himself away from the desk. The man, of course, was shocked to see that Father Bert in that condition. Bert looked at him, and said: "You know, I've listened to your arguments and I've concluded that they have merit. In fact, I don't have a leg to stand on!" In the final analysis, when you think about it, none of us do. We are all dependent, finally, on God and God's providence.

The gospel of Jesus Christ urges us to recognize that we are free persons and responsible. We are or should be responsible for who we are, who we become, what we do or don't do, what we say or don't say. We shape our lives and must take responsibility for those lives. We ought not to whine or blame others or surrender to self-pity or feel sorry for ourselves when things don't go right. The gospel of Jesus Christ also urges us to recognize something else. While responsible, we are not in ultimate control of our lives. We are not independent of or exempt from God's providence. There is a saying that asserts that no one knows enough to be a pessimist. One could also say that no one knows enough to distrust. No one knows enough not to have to let go, to surrender, to rely on God, to trust in providence.

A very common and primal human experience is fear and worry. Depending upon temperament, some worry a whole lot while others worry less. We can all probably make some kind of list of the things we fear and worry about. We worry about money or acceptance or failure or career or relationships. We worry about health and safety for ourselves and our loved ones. We worry about security and the future and happiness – happiness for ourselves and those we love. We fear and worry about a variety of things for ourselves and for others, but when you think about it we don't really have much or at times any control over a lot of things.

The gospel's message is don't worry, do not be afraid, trust. We are cared for by a loving providential God who is Father, Son, and Holy Spirit. Jesus reveals this caring providential God to us. He tells us: "Do not be afraid

— not even one sparrow falls to the ground without the Father's knowledge. You are worth more than sparrows." (Matthew 10:29, 30) Trust me. He says: "Don't worry — look at the birds of the air — they do not sew or reap or gather into barns, yet your heavenly Father feeds them. Are you not worth more? Are you not more important than they? Trust me." He says: "Don't worry — by worrying can any of you add one inch to your height or one moment to your life span? Trust me." He says: "Do not be afraid — even the hairs on your head are counted, so trust me." (Matthew 6:26-28)

To say "do not be afraid" and "don't worry" is easier said than done. The virtue of trust does not mean that we give up or that we surrender to the inevitable. It does not mean positive acquiescence to some fate or curse. To trust is to responsibly embrace and accept dependence and at times powerlessness, relying confidently on the goodness and care of a God who reveals self in Jesus through the Spirit to be a lovesick Father.

The message of Jesus is that God does not forget us, ignore us, abandon us. The message of Jesus is that God providentially is there, part of our lives, caring and loving. Even when we forget that or when we simply don't understand God's plan or when, in fact, we really want it to be a different plan, God's providence is God's loving, unfolding, existential plan for each of us. Our response to that ought to be and can be trust. To the degree that we trust God, to the degree that we grow in our trust, to that degree our worries can lessen.

There is a story of an Irish pastor who decided to tour his parish. Walking along a road in the countryside, he came across a very old man saying his prayers besides a roadside shrine to the Blessed Mother. The pastor was impressed, stopped, and said to the old man: "You must be very close to God." The man thought for a moment and then smiled, and said to the pastor: "Yes, Father, as a as a matter of fact, he is very fond of me!" The message of the gospel of Jesus Christ is that God is indeed very fond of each one of us. You can bet on that. You can trust!

XI

HUMILITY

The Los Angeles Times published a story not so long ago. A plane had been canceled and there was a long line of travelers at a counter trying to get on another flight. One man in line grew very impatient and pushed ahead of everyone else. He demanded a first class ticket on the next flight. The attendant told him that he would have to take care of other people on the line ahead of him. She asked that the man return to his place. The man, however, pounded on the counter and asked: "Do you have any have idea who I am?" The ticket agent immediately picked up the microphone and said: "Attention please, attention please, there is a gentleman at the ticket counter who doesn't know who he is. If anyone can identify him please come to the counter." The man immediately retreated to his place on line and everyone else applauded the attendant.

We sometimes jokingly refer to a psychiatrist as a "head shrinker." Perhaps we do that because we realize that when someone gets too big of a head, there might indeed be something not quite right.

In Vienna, Austria, there is a Franciscan church where the Hapsburgs, the Austrian royal family, are buried. There was a special ritual used in their funerals. When the procession reached the church, the lead mourner would knock on the door. A priest would ask: "Who desires admission here?" A guard would respond: "His apostolic majesty, the Emperor." The priest would answer: "I do not know him." The guard would knock a second time and announce the deceased to be the highest emperor. Again, the response from the priest was, "I do not know him." Finally, a third knock would provoke the same question from the priest: "Who desires admission here?" Then the answer would be: "The deceased is a poor sinner, your brother!" Then the door of the church would be opened.

Can you name ten humble people? Can you name five humble people? Does humility have any appeal today at all? Is it an attractive lifestyle? Does life in the business world, industry, entertainment, educational or athletic worlds offer any model for humility?

Humility is a virtue. It is about self-control and self-restraint. It is part of the virtue of temperance and moderates the drive to assert oneself. It breaks the slide into the world of egoism and self-promotion. In a very real sense we can become addicted to ourselves and our own interests, image or agenda. Narcissism beckons. But because humility is a virtue a woman or man who possesses it almost always acts with a sane, balanced, and sensible view about themselves. Humility is an inner attitude that candidly allows one to know oneself, love oneself, accept oneself. A person with humility sees their talent and accomplishments as gifts and recognizes their limits and failures as opportunities to become better, saner, and holier.

T.S. Elliot writes in his work, The Cocktail Party: "Half the harm that is done in this world is done by people who want to feel important. They don't mean to do harm – but the harm does not interest them, or they do not see it, or they justify it – because they are absorbed in the endless struggle to think well of themselves." Humility puts all that in perspective and allows us to see ourselves honestly. It enables us to clearly appraise and temper our self-confidence, self-reliance, self-seeking. In a word it gives us a balanced and sensible way of seeing ourselves.

Does the world we live in appreciate a humble person? Does our culture esteem humility? Is humility perceived to be simply a lack of get up and go? Is a humble woman or man perceived to be a loser? Are we trapped in a psycho-social world that is addicted to the ego? The world of the gospel is a counter-cultural world. The woman or man who accepts the gospel as a program for life simply plays by a different set of rules. Jesus tells us: "Learn from me for I am meek and humble of heart." (Matthew 11:29) Jesus also tells us: "He or she who exalts self shall be humbled and he or she who humbles self shall be exalted." (Luke 18: 14)

Each of us rightly should be concerned with self-preservation, which entails not only a concern for survival but also a concern for our good name, our professional status, our relationships with others. Obsessive concern for such things, however, results in pride. We wrap ourselves tighter and tighter into our own self and cut off others, the world, and reality. We strike out with no restraint at any threat to our own self-importance. It is really a pretty awful way to live, because it is based on a lie. We simply just do not know who we are nor can we accept who we are.

It is said that humility is lowliness which become selflessness. Lowliness does not mean depreciation of self, a debasement, neuroses nor masochism. It is not an inferiority complex. As the proverb states: A truly humble person does not think little of himself or herself; rather he or she thinks of himself or herself little. Humility is a virtue or disposition that allows one to love the self with no pretenses. A humble person is not ashamed of their humanity nor of the fact that as persons they have limits, faults, and negative features in need of healing and correction. The virtue of humility frees a person to be themselves, frees a person to face the need for growth and personal change. Humility frees someone from the need or compulsion to wear a mask and pretend to be someone else. It frees us to be willing to be what we are and to do what we can.

A willingness to be what we are! We are all dependent. Only the egoistical and self-centered fail to recognize their need for others and ultimately their need for God. We are all limited in some way. By nature and nurture we have boundaries and edges. We are, in fact, all of us sinners. Negative, dark drives surge up within us. The playwright, Eugene O'Neil, put it this way: "I am born broken and in need of glue."

We do what we can! As we truly come to know ourselves, and this takes a lifetime and a lot of work, we learn what we can and cannot do as well as what is and what is not worth doing. We do not have to do it all. We don't always have to get it right and we don't always have to do it by ourselves. A humble woman or man is a generous realist. They do not need to compete always or win always or beat up someone else. Nor do they need to succumb to despair. A humble person is not an unreasonable idealist. At the same time, humility does not mean mediocrity. Humility is the willingness to be what we are and to do what we can. It engenders a wise understanding and appreciation of self and that awareness brings peace. A long time ago St. Paul wrote a letter to the Christian community at Phillipi, in which he gave them advice. Paul was writing from his prison cell. He was disgraced and embarrassed, weak and powerless, and according to all appearances, a nobody. Yet this great Apostle urged his brothers and sisters in Christ to:

> ...humbly regard others as more important than yourselves, each looking out not for his own interests ... . have among yourselves the same attitude that is also yours in Christ Jesus, who, though he was in the form of God, did not regard equality with God something to be grasped. Rather he emptied himself, taking the form of a slave, coming in human likeness; and found human in appearance, he humbled himself, becoming obedient to death, even death on a cross. (Philippians 2:5-9)

That's not bad advice even for us today!

XII

GENTLENESS I

As is probably always the case everywhere, malls become jammed packed at Christmas time. This past year I went to a nearby mall to do Christmas shopping. When I was finished, I returned to my car and began to make my way out of the mall parking lot to the highway. Traffic was backed up for at least half a mile. We moved forward in inches. I looked in the rearview mirror and saw the driver behind me. It looked like he was furious. He kept leaning on his horn and getting redder in the face by the minute. This went on for some time until finally he bumped my car. By that time I had had it. I put on the brake, got out of the car, and stormed back to confront him. As I approached, he furiously rolled down the window, looked out, and saw me standing there wearing my Roman collar. He let out a moan and said: "Oh, my God." My response to him was: "Close but no cigar." The man, of course, had become enraged, furious, angry, bordering on violent. He had lost control. His parking lot rage is but one form of what seems to be increasing rage on almost every front. Violence, not legitimate self-defense, is evil and harms the self or another. Rage can take many different forms in many different degrees. It is no longer an uncommon experience in our world and in our culture. But for the life of me, I cannot see one positive thing that it ever accomplishes. In fact, violence or rage or uncontrolled anger in word or action just destroys, hurts, crushes, victimizes. The opposite of violence is nonviolence or gentleness.

Eugene Ionesco portrays a scene in one of his plays. A man comes home from work and sits down to eat his soup. There's a fly in the soup. He starts violently yelling at his wife, who yells back. The children join in, taking sides. Relatives living next door join in the violence by word and action. Soon the whole town is in an uproar and that provokes the neighboring town. The whole scene ends with a TV shot showing the whole world disintegrating in an atomic explosion. And it all began with a fly in the soup! Violence is certainly not new to human experience. However, the prevalence of violence today on all fronts seems to be different. The drive to extend the barriers of what is acceptable in terms of brutality seems to have an anesthetizing effect on many of us so that things that in another age were unthinkable are today merely ordinary and regular occurrences. So we see rage in many disguises portrayed on TV, in the movies, in print journalism, and we meet it on the streets and in our neighborhoods.

The prophet Zechariah, once spoke to Israel about the future coming of the Messiah, who would be a Prince of Peace, who would banish violence and rage. The Messiah would come humbly and with gentleness, riding on a colt, the fold of a donkey. Later, all the gospel writers would quote that passage to describe Jesus' triumphal entry into Jerusalem on Palm Sunday – just days before he would be violently assassinated on the cross. Jesus described himself in terms of nonviolence, in terms of gentleness. He tells us: "Learn from me for I am meek and gentle and humble of heart – you will find rest – my yoke is easy." (Matthew 11:28-30) Jesus repeats this in the Sermon on the Mount, where the second beatitude reads: "Blessed are the gentle, they shall inherit the land." (Matthew 5:4) St. Paul writes to the Corinthians: "I entreat you by the gentleness of Christ" and to the Christian community at Colossus and Ephesus he writes: "Put on as Christ's chosen ones, kindness and gentleness." (Colossians 3:12-13) The virtue of gentleness or meekness is a quality of God and of Jesus and a necessary quality for those who would follow Christ.

The virtue of gentleness is not weakness or cowardice. It is not submission. It is rather the interior power, force, the discipline to master self. Gentleness is the power to respond to violence with calm balance, inner strength and control. It is the ability to overcome the drive to get even, to strike out, to retaliate or escalate the level of rage. The virtue of gentleness or meekness refuses to be drawn into sterile arguments, to get the last word, to win out by beating someone else. Gentleness tempers and informs our behavior. It includes notions of compassion, forgiveness, generosity and kindness. The virtue of gentleness may not at first or in fact ever change an oppressive other. But it will do something to the hearts and souls of those who practice it. This virtue will give self-respect and inner harmony. It is a way to find that deep peace that can only come when conflict is either resolved charitably or simply rejected. Jesus tells us: "I am meek and humble of heart – learn from me, and you will find rest." It's pretty clear that a follower of Jesus is called to be non-violent, to be gentle with others and with oneself and to work to make gentle the life of the world. Are you gentle? Is your own part of the world gentle? In what you say and what you do is violence diminished? Jesus promises to those who are gentle the gift of peace and rest. He promises that the gentle among us will inherit the Kingdom of God.

XIII

GENTLENESS II

A teacher told this story. Every Christmas his students gave him a token gift. You could tell from the box what the gift was – handkerchiefs. It got to the point that this teacher would just put the boxes in his closet until he needed a new handkerchief. One day, months after Christmas, he opened the box to find an antique pocket watch. He had it all the time but didn't know it.

I suspect that we are all more than we know. There is more to who we are than we even suspect. We are spiritual persons. James Joyce, the Irish author, once wrote: "Mr. Duffy lived a short distance from his body." By that he meant that Mr. Duffy just simply had no awareness of who he was.

I think that we have the choice, and grace is not lacking, to be either small souled persons or great souled persons. We can be petty or magnanimous; we can settle for what we see in the mirror or we can stretch. When we realize who or what we can become and reach for it, we begin to glimpse the work of art that we are. We meet our gentle self.

One of the basic styles of a small souled person is aggression. Recently I witnessed bicycle rage. Of course, there are other forms of rage. There is sidewalk rage, shopper rage, taxi rage. There is also paranoia rage, conspiracy rage, "not getting your own way" rage. There is even rage about rage. When the ego has made itself central to the universe, then all things and all people are potential or actual rivals. The chronic attitude of this kind of person is suspicion. Life is about beating others and winning or at least always watching your back. A gentle, meek person controls their aggression and anger. Life's ups and downs are accepted as part of life. The gentle believe in goodness, growth, grace and self-discipline in the face of any challenge or calamity. St. Thomas Aquinas tells us that the virtue of gentleness makes us self-possessed. It never falls into a blind rage and does not get obsessed with revenge.

A wise guy has said: "It's not the earth the gentle or meek inherit, it's the dirt." I guess whoever said that has not yet climbed into the very essence of their spiritual self. Jesus tells us that the gentle or meek will in effect inherit the earth. The small souled think that only the tough, the pushy, the bullies inherit the earth. Gentleness suggests that when the soul is rooted in God, it need not be afraid or upset or off balance or out of control. It can rest easy believing that whatever might come, it is safe in the palm of God's hand. The gentle person inherits the earth. They can fearlessly reach out in love to others because others are simply not viewed as competitors but rather as friends. The gentle soul is rooted in profound peace, calm, and self-acceptance and so can walk the earth without envy or defensiveness, without recourse to rage as a lifestyle. Blessed are the gentle because the odds are that they will inherit the earth. At least that is the word of the Lord.

XIV

LOYALTY

The late spiritual writer Henri Nouwen has written a masterful meditation on Rembrandt's painting, "The Prodigal Son". Hanging in the Hermitage Museum in St. Petersburg, Russia, the painting portrays an elderly, half blind father embracing his returned and repentant son. Another son and brother passively witnesses the welcome home. For Rembrandt the father is the main character and centerpiece – some say the artist was painting himself – an aged man, worn out, burdened by life yet caring, accepting, forgiving. The parable and its artistic rendition suggest many virtues. One certainly is the virtue of loyalty or faithfulness. The prodigal father had remained loyal to his son who had abandoned him and loyal as well to the other son who stayed home but failed to understand him.

Jesus' parable in Luke's gospel of the prodigal son is meant to teach how loyal and faithful God is to his people (Luke 15:11-31). In fact, just about all the parables, miracles, teachings and history found in the New Testament, and perhaps in the whole Bible, tell the same story. No matter what happens God stays with us and stays for us, can be counted on, is faithful and loyal, never gives up on us, even when we don't deserve it. God is simply there for us. That loyalty ought to be mutual.

To be loyal or faithful is to be dependable, constant, steadfast. The faithful woman or man is there and can be counted on. Loyalty means remaining true. A mature person in freedom embraces their commitment, accepts responsibility for a commitment, and does so with constancy and reliability. The great King Solomon of the Hebrew Bible lamented: "Many a man (or woman) claims to have unfailing love, but who can find a faithful man (or woman) (Proverbs 20:6)." A culture or individual who has become cynical, suspicious or arrogant doesn't understand loyalty. For anyone of character, for anyone with competence at human living, rightly placed loyalty is a must. The antithesis of loyalty is alienation or estrangement – you can't be counted on to be there or you don't expect anyone to be there for you.

The ancient rabbis tell the story of two brothers. Both worked a farm together and shared everything that they produced and earned. One was single and the other married with children. One day the single brother thought to himself that things were not fair. "My brother has many needs which I do not." So every night that brother would bring a sack of grain across the field and dumped that grain in his brother's bin. About the same time the married brother began thinking that his single brother, being all alone, had needs that he did not. He thought it was not right and so every night he began to sneak across the field to dump a sack of grain in his brother's barn. This went on each night for years. Both, of course, were somewhat puzzled that their own grain supply never seemed to dwindle, but they did not question the miracle. One night both brothers set out at the same time and in the dark bumped into each other. At first they were startled but then it dawned on them what had been going on. They dropped their sacks of grain and hugged each other. The rabbis claimed that at that point the sky lit up and a voice from heaven spoke saying: "Here at last is the place where I will build my temple. For where brothers meet in love and loyalty and faithfulness there my presence shall dwell!"

Most of us are loyal, I am sure, to people, causes, institutions, and communities. St. Thomas Aquinas tells us that that is simply the way it should be. We owe faithfulness. It's the right thing to do especially to members of one's family (parents and siblings) and then to friends, to country or nation and to other special communities. So we owe loyalty to our Church. We owe it to God to be loyal to Him. We owe it in justice to be loyal and faithful to a number of others because we have received so much from them. It would be interesting to make a list of those persons and communities upon whom we depend to be the persons that we are. If we are not loyal and faithful we really, in a sense, lose touch with reality. We might begin to live with the fantasy that, in fact, we don't owe anyone anything.

While some virtues shape our social existence, loyalty is a virtue of personal reverence. It suggests deep respect and esteem mixed with affection and love toward others who have been so good to us. We venerate the objects of our faithfulness, especially our mothers and fathers, brothers and sisters. We venerate our Church. We venerate our nation. Faithfulness binds us over and over again to everyone and everything that is important and of value to our lives. Loyalty engenders genuine solidarity with those who are a necessary integral part of our lives, and it affects our attitudes and intentions toward them. Loyalty enables us to give of ourselves, to sacrifice and to be generous, to be grateful and supporting.

The great basketball coach at St. John's University in New York, Lou Carnesecca, held a press conference to announce his retirement from coaching. A reporter asked if he had lived by any motto or had any advice to share. Coach Carnesecca told the audience listening that when he had begun his coaching career his father had told him to always do two things. One was "to have deep pockets" and the other was "to be there." In a word his father had counseled him to be always loyal and faithful. Be there for God, for family, for friends, for Church, for country, for your own community. "Be there" is pretty good advice.

XV

COURAGE

It was very late at night and no one was on the street. A man was going home from work when he spotted someone coming toward him. He tensed as the other got closer. When the two were face to face on the darkened street the first man moved to the left in order to pass. At the same time the other made the same move. The two bumped into each other and then kept going. The first man began walking more quickly to his home. At the same time he reached back to check his wallet but it was gone. Furious, he turned around and ran after the other man. When he caught up with him he shouted: "Give me that wallet!" The other man handed over the wallet and then ran away. When our first man finally did get home, he unlocked the front door of his house, entered, went upstairs to the bedroom, turned on the light, and there saw his wallet on the bed. He had forgotten to take it with him when he left for work. It dawned on him, suddenly, that in fact he had just mugged someone. Fear can do strange things to us!

There are many things we fear on many and varied levels of life. Sometimes fear can make us desperate. We fear for ourselves and our loved ones. We fear sickness, accidents, violence, ruin and it is very understandable. We fear the loss of love, the rejection of love. We fear making commitments or we fear not having them and all of that is very understandable. We fear failing or being perceived of as failures on an economic, social, personal or relational level. We fear death and all the little forms that death takes during life and all of that is very understandable. On October 22nd, 1978, Pope John Paul II, began his ministry as universal pastor of the Catholic Church. His message on that day in St. Peter's Square was, "Be not afraid!" And in a real sense it was the organizing theme of his whole ministry. Of course, the Pope's call reflects the words of Jesus who counsels over and over again – be not afraid!

Courage is a virtue that is about fear and about strength. What it addresses, specifically, are all those things that get in the way of pursuing excellence and goodness. William Faulkner says in The Sound and the Fury that at times "life looks like the pieces of a broken mirror." For any number of reasons a man or a woman can be confronted with adversity, frustration, misfortune, desolation. We can be very afraid. Periods of darkness and disappointment and sorrow can overwhelm us, making it almost more than we can bear. We feel crushed and abandoned even by God. It is then that we have to be brave.

Perhaps today more than ever we need an culture of courage. Dr. Robert Coles, the Pulitzer prize author and psychiatrist, tells the story of a young African-American child, Ruby Bridges. The six year old was the first black child to attend an all white school in New Orleans, Louisiana, under a court order in 1960. Ruby was escorted daily to the school by federal marshals because the local and state police refused to protect her from an angry mob opposed to forced integration. Rather than finding a girl shattered by rejection, Dr. Coles tells us that he found a Christian child who prayed for her enemies. He tells us that at first he did not believe that she was really praying. He thought that somehow she was compensating for her fear and abnormal anxiety. The girl, however, told Dr. Coles that she would pray, "Please, God, try to forgive those people, 'cause they just don't know what they're doing."

Courage does not mean that we are never afraid. Bravery is action in spite of fear. What it means is that we hang on, fight, never give up, pursuing fullness of life and happiness while being afraid. Sometimes courage means coming to the rescue. It is daring. For instance, an elderly woman is saved from a fire. Most of the time, however, courage is quiet. It is simply enduring. The former is usually dramatic and suggests action; the latter, while not passive submission, is resolved firmness. We bear our suffering. Dr. Coles tells another story about the writer Walker Percy. Several of Percy's ancestors had committed suicide. Percy told Dr. Coles as he battled prostate cancer: "All my life I hoped I could die this way. Many times I thought of taking my life. I often thought of asking a doctor to help me. I'm glad and relieved I never did." Walker Percy with great bravery accepted his illness, and as Dr. Coles tell us, "He was waiting to be taken by Someone, with a capital 'S'."

The great St. Augustine has said: "Courage is love readily enduring all for the sake of what is loved!" It very much represents an overcoming of self or a stretching of self. Ultimately, the brave person takes responsibility for life. This is seen in great acts of heroism as well as in accepting the conflicts, sufferings, and challenges of ordinary living. It takes courage to suffer, endure, decide, act, accept, and not run away and hide.

A student of mine once asked me, "Why is life so hard?" She was referring to a host of issues, e.g. a career decision, pressures from family and self, relational difficulties. We talked for a while and it suddenly dawned on me that this student had been sold a bill of goods. She really thought that life was not supposed to be hard. The Philosopher Albert Camus once said, "Everyone over thirty is responsible for his or her face." By that he meant experience and the knocks of life age us. Most of us know that life is hard and that is inevitable. The virtue of courage enables and empowers us to accept life as it is in its totality and to work to change what can and should be changed. Courage is a radical act of freedom. It rejects death and all the little deaths that go with life. Courage always walks away from the tomb to resurrection. Jesus tells us over and over again: "Be not afraid."

Human living requires courage every minute to love, to feel, to be vulnerable, to live and be, to seek and speak truth, to know self, to be happy. W.B. Yeats put it this way: "Why should we honor those that die upon the fields of battle; a man or woman may show as reckless a courage in entering into the abyss of himself." A man or woman of courage is a moral hero. Bravery colors and fashions who they are and what they do. There is a certain nobility that the brave have which appeals to all. By their lives, they give testimony to the value of human life, the inevitability of eternal life, the possibility of human happiness. Courageous women and men call all of us to a vision of something grand and supremely worthwhile. No form of death for the brave is ever the final word. To repeat St. Augustine, "Courage is love, readily enduring all for the sake of what is loved."

XVI

HOSPITALITY

Moral exile is deliberate distance and separation from other human persons and is often measured by loneliness, defensiveness, aggressive or rude behavior. By nature we all seek social relationships or at least we should. The moral exile is alone, hiding behind a wall. Gruffness, unfriendliness, lack of hospitality is spiritual swindle. Such a person is fooling the other, fooling themselves, and in the long run will simply shrivel. Obviously, there are a variety of degrees and ways of inhospitality. Eventually, however, it all boils down to the same thing – moral exile.

But, and here is the rub, we owe it to ourselves and to others to be friendly and hospitable. We owe it to others and ourselves to be pleasant, agreeable, open, and sincere. It is a debt of honor that our very integrity requires. Women and men must live together and with each other on a variety of different levels and to different degrees of intensity and that demands civility and friendliness. We simply cannot survive without hospitality. USA Today once reported that a woman psychologist in North Carolina had done a study and found that children smile on an average of four hundred times a day; adults only fifteen times a day. As we get older we become more guarded, less open, less spontaneous, more restrained. We become or can become inhospitable. Maybe it is a fear of rejection or misinterpretation. Maybe it is because we become more self-absorbed and walled in on ourselves. Maybe it's because we are afraid.

St. Thomas Aquinas tells us that friendliness or affability or hospitality is a virtue. It is something that we owe others in justice. The virtue of hospitality calls for a pattern of behavior that inclines us to be agreeable in word and actions with others. We deliberately try to be pleasant, amicable, courteous to other people, and we do this with all people and not just with those that we like or with those who are like us. The more frequently we act in a friendly, affable, hospitable way, the more we become that kind of person. Living in this way leads to a life of graciousness. Ultimately, we behave this way because each person is worthy of reverence no matter how they act toward us. A hospitable or affable person refuses to let someone else's obnoxiousness or rudeness control or manipulate their behavior. Because of the virtue of affability, a person is able to resist being victimized by those who are disagreeable. Luke's gospel is especially sensitive to Jesus' hospitality and affability toward others. For instance, in that gospel we read that at least on nine occasions Jesus had dinner with other people. The kingdom of God is compared to a hospitable, affable banquet. We read that on two occasions Jesus ate with members of his own community. On two other occasions he ate with tax collectors. On three occasions he ate with Pharisees. Jesus then compares the coming kingdom of God to banquets, and in fact, the rich man who refused hospitality is condemned. Hospitality is displayed by Jesus in other contexts as well. He displays a warmth which welcomes the sinner, the stranger, the family member, the friend. Jesus displays gestures of affability and friendship. He even welcomes the repentant thief into paradise as he himself dies because of the brutality of others.

Life on the streets, in the office, on trains or buses, on highways or at home can be filled with irritants and annoyances and a certain harshness. If we are going to live together we disparately need to be affable, friendly, and courteous to each other. This behavior is simply owed to others. The virtue of hospitality suggests that we approach others with thoughtfulness for their feelings and with care. Such respectable behavior gives style and class to life and begins to build a civilization of love. Words, gestures, and actions express sensitivity and mutual respect for another person who is seen as an image of God himself. While other virtues may address the larger issues of life, hospitality and friendliness address the everyday, ordinary interactions and exchanges among people. And that can make all the difference in the world!

XVII

KINDNESS

For a number of years I have shown my students the film on the life of Mother Teresa made by the Petrie sisters. The film is truly inspirational and very well done. What always stays with me after a showing, of course, is that remarkable face of Mother Teresa. When she ministers to a dying outcast in India, when she strokes the face of a disabled senior citizen, when she caresses a sick infant, there is something that shines through her face. As I say, that image stays with me for days. A few years ago having seen the film a number of times I had the chance of meeting Mother Teresa in person. I had been teaching some of her seminarians in Rome. Mother Teresa came to that city to accept the vows of her sisters. After a joyous concelebrated Mass, Mother came to the sacristy to greet the priests. I spoke with her briefly and held her hand. As I looked into her face, I recognized the image I had seen so often before in the Petrie film. What shown through, what I saw in that small face was kindness.

The gospel tells us that Jesus' mission was to proclaim and inaugurate the kingdom of God. The kingdom of God is, of course, religious language and a Biblical metaphor. It is meant to suggest a new order, a new world, a new creation, a new way of being a human person. It is not meant to suggest an idealized utopia that is simply un-attainable. Rather, the "kingdom of God" metaphor con-notes the transformation of the world – "Thy kingdom come on earth as it is in heaven." We and the whole world have been redeemed, rescued, converted, saved, trans-formed. All of creation and all of human existence takes its meaning from a vibrant relationship to Mystery, the mystery who is our God, Father, Son and Holy Spirit. The mystery of God is Emmanuel – God with us. We breathe grace and live a new life. One could say that the kingdom of God is the life of kindness. John Ruskin, the English au-thor, tells a story. One day he was sitting in a house looking out a window. The window faced down on a valley. As sun set, Ruskin could see the torch of a lamplighter lighting street lamps. Because of the darkness he could not see the lamplighter himself, only the torch and the dots of light it left behind. Ruskin commented to a friend: "That's like a Christian. People may never know him or her, meet or see him or her, but they know a Christian has passed through their world by the trail of light they leave behind them." That trail of light is characterized by a number of differ-ent virtues. But probably all those character traits could be distilled into one and that one is kindness. Kindness is the full flowering of all the human virtues. George Eliot once described the world as being characterized by, "an unre-flective egoism," a world filled with people who tell lies about themselves and at times believe the lies. Kindness is just the opposite. Kindness is unreflective loving. The vir-tue of kindness is connected to the virtue of charity. It is, in fact, charity or love in action. Genuine loving requires in the words of Pascal "reasons that reason knows not of." Kindness takes that love and puts it into practical concrete action. Kindness does good things to others. Kindness offers gestures of compassion, words and actions that are truly and effectively helpful. Kindness is gentleness and sympathetic understanding; it is generous conduct and it is generous speech. Because kindness is a virtue, it is a kind of ingrained disposition. It becomes second nature to us to do kind things. Of course, to become a kind person takes practice and it takes a lot of work. We have to want to be kind. Kindness implies respect and reverence for another person. It is an antidote to pettiness and mean spiritedness. Kindness, in a word, makes us to be better and more humane. It really is a sign of the kingdom of God on earth. Where kindness flourishes, the world becomes new, more complete, a lot better and a whole lot more than one dreamt possible.

I was once walking on Fifth Avenue in New York City. A homeless person sat on the steps of a building begging for money. I was about to walk on, not even paying attention. At that moment a messenger on a bicycle also passed by. The man was making some kind of a delivery. As he pedaled up the avenue, he spotted the homeless person. He braked, picked up his bike, crossed the sidewalk and gave the woman a dollar. As I watched I was edified by the kindness of the messenger who had deliberately stopped to help someone in need. I was also ashamed that I had almost passed by without noticing someone in need. I wondered how often I had done that in the past. The world would perish without kindness. The kind person passes through the world leaving a trail of light behind them.

XVIII

COMPASSION

Steven Covey in his very popular book, The Seven Habits of Highly Effective People, tells a story. One Sunday morning he, Covey, got on a subway train in New York City. He began reading a newspaper while other people either dozed or were lost in their own thoughts. At one station a man with three children boarded the train. Very soon the children were playing, yelling, running, and in effect disturbing the other passengers. The father seemed oblivious to what was happening. The children continued to annoy the other passengers until finally Covey decided to do something about it. He went to the father and said: "Sir, can you did something to control your children?" The father seemed to come out of a daze and become aware for the first time about what was happening. He began to explain to Covey that he and his children had just come from the hospital where the children's mother had just died. He and they really did not know how to handle what had happened. Covey tells us that immediately he saw things differently, and because he saw things differently, he began to feel differently. And because he began to feel differently, he began to be behave differently. He tells us: "My irritation vanished, I didn't have to worry about controlling my attitude or my behavior; my heart was filled with the man's pain. Feelings of sympathy and compassion flowed freely." Covey could only ask what he could do to help. Everything had changed for him in an instant.

The word compassion is a translation of the Hebrew word, "rahamim," the plural form for the word meaning, "womb." That Hebrew word for compassion literally means "trembling womb". What it suggests is a tender care and concern as a mother or father would have for their child. Compassion comes from two Latin words "cum" and "passio" which literally means "to suffer with."

The great North African bishop St. Augustine defines the virtue of compassion as the heartfelt identification with another person's pain or distress, driving us to do what we can to help. The ancient Greek philosopher Aristotle claimed that compassion was especially called for when misfortune afflicts a person who has not deserved it. Compassion is a feeling for someone in need. We resonate with another's pain; we sympathize. It is a strong movement of the heart, but it is also an act of the will. The compassionate woman or man is moved deeply, and eventually is moved often or all the time by the pain of another. It becomes second nature to them to recognize suffering or to sense it. All of us know the range of human hurt and, while it is pretty broad, it is not always obvious. The virtue of compassion equips a person to catch on, to be aware, to be moved deeply by someone else's suffering. In a very real way, a compassionate person makes that pain their own. But that's not all. The compassionate woman or man then dives in and works to make things better.

The virtue of compassion allows someone to become skilled at detecting hurt, seeing or sensing the need of another. What another is going through really moves a person. They become vulnerable to the needs of another. There is a sensitivity, a tenderness, an empathy to the plight of another. A compassionate person literally takes on and makes their own the painful situation of another. Compassionate people put themselves in another's place. They walk in the shoes of another. They do it in the final analysis because the other person is a human person and in some sense viewed as a friend. St. Thomas Aquinas puts it this way: "... to one who loves, a friend is but another self, and so counts the friend's misfortunes as their own and grieves over them in the same way." A person is moved to compassion not only at the hurt of a friend but also at that of a stranger. This happens because at some point we either have been or could be in the same situation and can know the same feeling of desperation.

The gospel offers us a portrait of Jesus as the most compassionate of men, the most compassionate God. Story after story, word after word show Jesus as deeply feeling the pain of others, sensing their needs or hurts and then doing something about them. Jesus once saw a funeral procession leaving the small village of Naim. A young man had died, the only son of a widowed mother. The gospel tells us that Jesus raised him from the dead and then tenderly gave him back to his mother. On another occasion an official of the synagogue desperately begged Jesus to heal his teenage daughter. When Jesus arrived at the house, a crowd of people were in mourning because the child had died. Jesus raised that young woman from the dead and gave her back to her father. Two sisters lost their brother, a friend of Jesus. Jesus raised Lazarus from the dead and gave him back to his sisters. Jesus felt compassion for the hungry and fed them, for the thirsty and quenched that thirst, for the lost and the confused and for so many others. To them all, Jesus was compassionate — a man of compassion, a God of compassion.

Compassion ultimately is about action or behavior. It is about doing something concrete and effective to help someone in need. You try to fix things or to make them better or at least to lessen the pain that someone is going through. Hurt and pain are an inevitable part of the human experience. Not to know that or not to accept that is to either be in denial or not to have lived very long. But simply to tolerate or stoically bear hurt is not acceptable. The virtue of compassion moves against complacency, indifference, abandonment, and isolation. Compassion, in fact, builds community, solidarity, and a culture of sympathy. It is not the experience of pain that determines the quality of our lives. Rather it is how we deal with that pain and hurt, our own or that of another and what we do about it that signals how noble our lives are. The virtue of compassion leads to that nobility.

XIX

MERCY

The Bay of Naples in Italy is the habitat of a jellyfish called Medusa and of a snail of the Nudibranch variety. When the snail is small the jellyfish sometimes swallows it and draws it into its digestive tract. The snail, of course, is protected by a hard shell and so can't be digested. It fastens itself to the inside of the jellyfish and very slowly begins to eat it from inside out. By the time the snail is fully grown, it has consumed the entire jellyfish.

The Holy Spirit living in us can consume us, transform us from within. We can become people we never dreamt of becoming. We can become great souled people. We can become virtuous people. We can become women and men of mercy and in many ways mercy is the fundamental expression of the great souled. Mercy comes from the Latin word, misericordia, which literally means a sorrowful heart. Mercy, therefore, is compassionate understanding of another's unhappiness. A person is merciful when he or she feels the sorrow and the misery of another as if it were their own and tries to do something about it. The great St. Bernard once said: "If mercy were a sin, I believe I could not keep from committing it." Through mercy and compassion a person is redeemed. Mercy and redemption are not won or gained or bought. Mercy and redemption are not deserved. Mercy and redemption are not expected and come as a surprise. Mercy and redemption respect justice but go beyond it. Mercy and redemption, when offered, can set a person free to be born again, to start over, to find new life.

Mercy or redemption doesn't always make sense at least to some. A preacher once played with the gospel parable of the prodigal son and in his homily changed Jesus' whole story. He was trying to make a point. He had the father embrace the older brother, not the returned runaway. The father put a robe and ring on the older son and held a feast for him in gratitude for that son's hard work and faithfulness. He ignored the returned runaway. At that point in his homily a man in the back of the church stood up and yelled: "That's the way Jesus should have told the story!" Mercy doesn't make sense to some.

Mercy is compassion shown to an offender, clemency given instead of severity. It is deliverance, escape, release, a favor or blessing. The virtue of mercy or redemption, of course, must live side by side with other virtues such as justice, wisdom, common sense. It is intricately tied in with compassion and therefore with the virtue of charity or love. Mercy is a developed disposition or inclination to give someone a break. Thomas Aquinas, the medieval theologian, can say, "Mercy does not destroy justice but fulfills it." Mercy without justice is a kind of illusion; justice without mercy can be cruelty or simply revenge.

The gospel is a story of mercy and redemption. It tells us that God "desires mercy not sacrifice" (Matthew 9:13). It tells us, "be merciful as your heavenly father is merciful." (Luke 6:36) It tells us, "Blessed are the merciful for they shall obtain mercy." (Matthew 5:7)

Mercy or redemptive generosity is a virtue that allows us to see someone who is unfortunate and in some kind of need but in a new way. It gives a new scope to generosity. The merciful reach out, not in arrogance or snobbishness or smugness. A merciful woman or man chooses to act and does so almost automatically. Such a person assumes the responsibility to promote the real good of another, whether they deserve that kind of treatment or not. And often enough it is in fact not deserved or merited. The Christian corporal and spiritual works of mercy have nothing to do with whether someone is worthy or not.

All religions and spiritual traditions come together in their insistence upon mercy. It is a constant theme of Jesus' teaching. To focus especially on oneself simply shrinks a human person. We become diminished and it dwarfs us. It leads to pretty narrow, constricted, unfinished lives. That's to be expected because living like that, being that kind of a person, wrapped in self, is only a facsimile of who we are meant to be. Our self-identity expands to include others when we are merciful. Mercy can become the simple expression of the deepest truth about ourselves.

A study in Holland was done some time ago of those women and men who had saved Jews from the Nazis during the Holocaust. In almost every instance these good people, these "righteous Gentiles," had acted spontaneously with no agonizing decision about what they should do. They took Jews into their homes and hid them there or wherever they could. They did it because that was the kind of people they were. That was their truth. One said: "We are Christians, we had to help." They were moved as persons in the depths of their being by the power of mercy. When we are moved by generosity, graciousness, compassion, mercy, it feels like a release of something that is pent up in us. We are that way because it's right. The great souled person, the spiritually conscious person, knows intuitively their inescapable connectedness to others. Mercy, generous giving beyond what is owed, is not simply an ethical command. It is a behavioral and attitudinal realization that in Christ all, especially the least or little ones, are my brothers and sisters. And in some way what happens to them happens to me. The virtue of mercy, redemption, undeserved generosity can help tame our basic, more primitive instincts. It can help us see ourselves and know ourselves the way God knows us. And it can help us go through life as ministers of redemption. Mercy shows us that God loves us because of who God is, not because of who we are. Categories of worthiness do not apply. Blessed are the merciful for they shall receive mercy.

XX

HOPE

In one of her works Annie Dillard writes about a weasel. We think of a weasel often as slippery as when a person "weasels out" of something or escapes or slinks away. Annie Dillard has another take on the weasel and tells the story of an eagle that attacked a weasel. In defending itself, the weasel dug its teeth into the throat of the eagle. The author graphically describes the flight of the eagle with its talons trying to tear the body of the weasel away from its throat. Some years later the skeleton of the eagle was found. The head of the weasel was still embedded in its throat.

Perhaps the weasel can serve as a metaphor for God's commitment to us. God simply never lets us go. God is our hope. It is the nature of God to honor commitments, to stay with us, to be obviously reliable. The English poet Francis Thompson used the metaphor of a hound – the Hound of Heaven – to convey the same truth. The clinging power of the weasel can indeed suggest not only God's reliability, but it can also describe our own trust and hope. Hope is a virtue about a future good for oneself or another. It is not just a wish but a desire accompanied by expectation. There is something I want and do not have and there is a good reason to believe that I might get what I want. Hope is about imagining the future, wishing intensely for the unseen and hanging in there no matter what. It is a force that colors my attitude toward life itself. There are three movements to the virtue of hope. The first is that you really want something which you do not have and that to a degree relativizes other wants. Second, it may be difficult to get what you want but you are confident about achieving that goal. The third moment in hope is that you are convinced that what you're looking for is attainable and therefore you go for it with enthusiasm. People of hope have a positive view of life and so obstacles or impediments are viewed as simply normal and to be expected. Rather than give up and quit, hopeful people devise a number of strategies or routes that they can take to realize their objective. Hope, therefore, involves wishing strongly. It also means that in order to get what I want I may need the help of others. Hope therefore issues into a community of friends. The virtue of hope of course involves waiting. We simply refuse to quit. We tough it out. We wait.

Hopeful people are not naive. They see clearly beyond the shadows to possibilities. They take responsibility for the future and channel it to the extent possible. The Vietnamese Buddhist monk, Thich Nhat Han, has written: "One can choose to be watering the seeds of happiness, rather than those of discontent." A person of hope may have their back to the wall but always sees a possibility that is not yet realized. They see a way around their troubles. The virtue of hope engenders strength of spirit. It equips a person to deal with setbacks even in the face of depression and on the brink of despair. Hope stays fixed on a goal and a promise and is always ready to move forward when an opportunity presents itself. Hope, like all virtues, comes with practice and with grace. We choose to be hopeful rather than surrender to defeat. We do this as often as we can. At times it may seem that we hope against hope.

Annie Dillard's weasel and Francis Thompson's hound might indeed be metaphors for the virtue of hope. Hope is a power, a strength, a solid rock.

Hope is a major theme of Biblical revelation. The hope the Bible talks about is, in fact, essential for human living. St. Paul often insists that we live by hope. He writes:

> For in hope we are saved. Now hope that is seen is not hope ... . but if we hope for what we do not see, we wait for it with patience ... . we know that in everything God works for good with those who love him ... . nothing will be able to separate us from the love of God in Christ Jesus. (Romans 8:24, 25, 28, 37-39)

The Letter to the Hebrews tells us that hope is like an anchor of the soul. We hope for many things but ultimately we hope for communion with God himself and the gift of peace or shalom. That is our destiny – completeness, harmony, fullness, abundance of life, happiness. Paul's First Letter to the Corinthians tells us that if we hope for this life only we are to be pitied because Christ really has been raised from the dead. The object of hope far exceeds anything that is less.

With hope we can hold out in the darkest moments. Sometimes that is just by the skin of our teeth but we just don't give up. Hope is a toughness that allows someone to go on no matter what. Hope fosters a dream about the future for each of us and for all of us which ultimately is the dream of life in abundance that Jesus promises.

A hopeful person reflects the simplicity of a child, a kind of purity that cannot abide pessimism and cynicism. To live with hope and trust is to live free from fear. It is to let the Spirit live in us, especially when we need it most, convinced that we are never alone or abandoned. The Irish poet, Seamus Heneay, in the Cure at Troy writes:

> History says, don't hope
> On this side of the grave. But then once
> In a lifetime
> The longed for tidal wave
> Of justice can rise up, and
> Hope and history rhyme!
> Believe that a further shore,
> Is reachable from here.

The hopeful person is convinced that a far shore is indeed reachable from here.

XXI

LOVE

Luis Untermeyer wrote a poem some years ago about coal miners in Wales. These miners would rise very early in the morning before the sun was up and went to work. When they arrived at their job site they boarded elevators and descended into the shafts. There they worked in semi-darkness almost all day long. When the day was over, they returned to the surface of the earth. By that time, however, the sun had set and so it was dark. They practically lived their entire life in the dark. The poet tells us that each evening these miners would ride the elevator back to the surface of the earth and they would pray together. They would say: "Oh, God if this night you love us, throw us a handful of stars!" If there is anything said in the Bible it is that God loves us. It is said over and over again. It is said in many different ways. And so perhaps life for us should be a constant search for those "handful of stars!"

Jesus tells us that we are created to love God and to love our neighbor as we love ourselves. We are loved into being to be a friend – God's friend, our own friend and friends with others. It's astonishing but true. John's gospel tells us: "For God so loved the world that he gave his only Son that whoever believes in him should not perish but have eternal life." (John 3:16) John also tells us in one of his letters: "This is how God showed his love among us: He sent his one and only Son into the world that we might live through him. This is love: Not that we loved God, but that he loved us and sent his Son as an atoning sacrifice for our sins. Dear friends, since God so loved us, we also ought to love one another." (I John 4:7-11)

Christian morality, Christian existence is centered on love. It's not about fear or manipulation or coercion. It's about love. The psychologist Rollo May, writing In Love and Will says: "Life comes from survival; but the good life comes from what we care about." The theological virtue of charity or love is a gift, a movement of love from God to us drawing us into friendship with God and solidarity and communion with others. That great poet of love, St. John, puts it this way: "God is love. Whoever loves dwells in God, and God in them. Those who claim to love, but hate their sisters and brothers are liars, because those who do not love people whom they can see, cannot love God whom they have not seen." (I John 4:16-20)

Love is many things. It is a feeling, an emotion, an attitude, a passion. Most of all, however, love is caring. St. Thomas Aquinas defines love as behavior. It is doing or willing good to another. Love of friendship, the virtue of charity, instills in us a disposition, a restlessness, a readiness to do good. To love is to go out of self or to die to self. There is in each of us a tendency to self-addiction or self-absorption. Theologians call this original sin. There is in each of us an inertia, an unwillingness to move beyond self-preoccupation. The virtue or grace of love helps us climb out of that cage or tomb. We reach out to others in love in a variety of ways. Ironically, when a woman or man loves this way, loves generously, is self-sacrificing, they, in fact, become more fully human, more complete as persons.

Love has a variety of expressions and objects. It can be the passion of married lovers, family ties, the bond between friends. Love can be a glance or word of encouragement; it can be a gift or donation. Love can be a helping hand or quiet support. In a word, a loving person looks for a way to make life better for the one they love.

"Charity begins at home" is one of those old cliches that does make a point. We must love ourselves and those immediately connected to us. Without doubt, we have faults or limits and we fail. But God loves us and so there is goodness in us. It is essential and psychologically healthy if we appreciate that. We are commanded to love others "as we love ourselves" (Mark 12:29, 29-31) and St. Paul tells us: "We are God's work of art created in Christ Jesus for the good works which God has already designated to make our way of life." (Ephesians 2:10) The Irish Dominican poet Fr. Paul Murray, OP, has written that God would die of unhappiness if anyone of us ceased to exist. How sad we don't let ourselves up; how sad we don't give ourselves a break!

We love our friends. Aristotle has defined a friend as two persons with one soul. We read great praise of friendship in the book of Ecclesiasticus (6:14-17): "Faithful friends are a sturdy shelter: Whoever finds one has found a treasure. Faithful friends are beyond price; no amount can balance their worth...." The columnist Walter Winchell would say: "A friend is someone who walks in when the rest of the world walks out!"

Friendship is most actual and intimate in marriage. It is a strong bond and relationship between two persons. Marriage is the process of becoming each other's best friend. Of course, it takes time and work and a whole lot of prayer. Potentially, friendship can extend and be offered widely. Ultimately, the virtue of charity or love can encompass everyone. Exclusion of people for whatever reason weakens love. Racism, for example, damages others but also victimizes the racist and deprives him or her of the holiness and harmony that love of others can bring.

Love is God's presence in us. St. John, again, tells us: "Whoever loves, dwells in God, and God in them!" (I John 4:16-20) What can you say about God and God's love? Let's just say that we can't do without it. Let's just say life would be so empty, so lonely, so frightening, so cold, without it. Let's just say that with it, I am healed, consoled, satisfied, accepted, at home. Let's just say, thank you! And let's give that unending gift of life to others. The lawyer in Luke's gospel asked Jesus: "What must he do to have life – unending life – life in abundance." The response Jesus gave was love – "love God with all your heart, soul, strength, and mind; love your neighbor as you love yourself." Jesus then added: "do this and you shall live!" (Luke 10:29-37)

XXII

FAIRNESS

Fyodor Dostoevsky tells a story about an onion. Once upon a time there was a peasant woman who was very wicked. One day she died leaving not a single good deed behind. The devils caught hold of her and plunged her into the lake of Hades. Her guardian angel stood by and wondered what good deed he could remember to tell God about. The angel mentioned, "Why, she once pulled up an onion from her garden and give it to a beggar woman."

And God replied, "You take that onion then, hold it out to her in the lake, and let her take hold of it and be pulled out by it. If you can pull her out of the lake of Hades, let her come into Paradise, but if the onion breaks, then the woman must stay where she is."

The angel ran to the woman and held out the onion toward her. "Come and catch hold," cried the angel "and I'll pull you out." So the angel began cautiously pulling her out. He had almost rescued her when the other sinners in the lake, seeing how she was being saved, began clutching at her legs so that they too could be pulled out. The wicked woman, however, began kicking at them. "I'm to be pulled out, not you. It's my onion, not yours. Let go." As soon as she uttered these words, the onion broke. The woman fell back into the lake of Hades where she remains to this day. And the guardian angel wept as he went away.

One could ask after reading this story whether it was fair. Did the woman deserve what she got? Was it just?

The human person is conscious of the self and responsible for the choices he or she makes. Those choices are made in liberty and freedom. At least that is true for most of us to varying degrees. We are who we decide to be! Yet, we don't do this alone. We don't journey through life in isolation. The poet John Dunne tells us, "No man is an island." So where we become truly ourselves is through relationships. The order and harmony that prevails among people, the style of relating is governed by the virtue of fairness or it is governed by the lack of fairness!

Some virtues e.g. self-control, are primarily concerned about shaping the individual person. Justice or fairness deals with our interaction with others. What ought to characterize our behavior toward others is fairness. This is fundamental for the human person and the human community.

Fairness or justice cannot be limited simply to what civil law demands. Many things may not be against the law but are unfair. It's unfair to discriminate against women or ethnic groups because of their gender or ethnicity, but it happens and in some places it's not even illegal. But it is unjust. Fairness or the virtue of justice is rooted in the transcendental nature of the human spirit. A person recognizes his or her solidarity with other human persons. That oneness requires that we treat one another with dignity and that we respect their rights. At the same time human solidarity impels us to be responsible in some way for the needs of others.

In his great work of theology, the *Summa Theologica*, Thomas Aquinas defines the virtue of justice as, "the strong and firm will to give to each his due." (II-II,

58, I) The German philosopher Emmanuel Kant states: "The other person may be in need or not, he may be in distress or not; but if it is a question of his right, then I am obliged to satisfy it." At times that is easier said than done. Distinctions need to be made. Sometimes fairness demands that I treat all with exact equality as in the exchange of goods and services. There is a kind of mathematical or absolute measure at work in the exchange. At other times, however, fairness needs to be proportional or geometric. Certain things are due to some that are not due to others. It's not just nice to care for the weak and feeble. It is required by justice. I am obliged. It is my obligation to treat those in need with fairness.

The nature of the human community asks that each person be just and seek justice. This is basic and elementary. It's not only a question of one on one relationships. Justice is not only about getting what I deserve. Fairness extends to seeing to it that others get what is rightfully theirs. Fairness or the virtue of justice impels a person to try to balance a number of relationships. It impels a person to seek the common good. The just person is truly a citizen of the whole world. Selfishness or egoism or isolation or demanding my fair share just doesn't cut it.

Is a just world order merely a dream? At times it would seem so. Justice and fairness, however, begin with how I treat others in my little part of the world. Do I give my "others" what is their due?

Justice allows us, empowers us to treat other people fairly. Because it is a virtue or because it becomes second nature a person does this with ease and style, and if not all the time, then most of the time. Fairness is a neighborly virtue, and when you think about it, is indispensable for life together on this planet. A just person treats others as equals and works for their common human good. Lack of fairness attacks the very fabric of human existence. It is anti-social. It reflects a contempt for others. The virtue of justice or fairness injects rationality into the way we relate to others. You can't live alone and you can't live with others without fairness.

XXIII

FORGIVENESS

Pope Benedict XVI declared Fr. Damian of Molakai to be a "saint". Fr. Damian was a Belgian priest who became a missionary to lepers or the victims of Hanson's disease on Molakai in the Hawaiian Islands. He worked for his people for many, many years. He served as a kind of doctor, nurse, judge, policeman, and of course, pastor. After twenty-five years on Molakai, Fr. Damian once began his homily with the words, "we lepers." He had contracted Hanson's disease. After his death, the city of Honolulu decided to honor his memory with a statue. They commissioned a Ms. Marisol Escobar to do the work. On the day the statue of Fr. Damian was unveiled there was some consternation. He is portrayed as a leper and so his physical features are ravaged. Ms. Escobar was interviewed and asked why she chose to feature the effects of the disease in her work. Her response was that what she had tried to capture was, "the mystery of personal transformation." Damian had become what he wanted to become – totally one with his people. The "mystery of personal transformation!"! The virtuous life is the path or way to personal transformation. It is the way to become the person you were meant to be. It is to become more than you ever dreamt of being. It is the way to become a saint. One of the many virtues or character traits needed for human completeness, for peace and happiness, is the virtue of forgiveness.

I once preached a homily on forgiveness in a local parish church. After Mass, a woman came up to speak with me. She was furious. She accused me and the church of laying a guilt trip on her. Her husband had walked out on her and the children leaving them with nothing. She was deeply hurt and angry. How could she forgive? The next week I preached at the same church. Without divulging the woman's identity, I explained what had happened the week before. I apologized for being unclear or for offending the woman. I did not mean to lay a guilt trip on anyone. My point though was twofold: The heart of the gospel of Jesus is forgiveness and refusal to forgive damages the one who refuses pardon more than it does the one who caused hurt.

There is no doubt about it, some people can really hurt others. Evil can be done by some to others. That hurt, whatever form it takes, causes pain, resentment and anger. Those feelings or emotions or reactions are very understandable and sometimes completely justified. To feel that way makes sense at least for a while. But if we refuse to forgive the one who hurts or offends us, does wrong by us, that refusal can poison us and not the offender. The Bible very clearly paints a portrait of forgiveness and the need to pardon. In the book of Genesis, we read how Abraham bargained with God, made a deal with God to win His forgiveness. Abraham asked God that if he could find fifty innocent people in the city, would God then still wipe out that place because of its evil? God told Abraham no. Abraham continued bargaining: What if I find forty-five innocent people, what if I find forty or thirty, what if they are only ten innocent people? God, will you still punish the city? The answer is that God would not punish and would forgive even if he doesn't find any innocent people. (Genesis 18:20-32)

In the New Testament St. Paul tells us: "Christ pardoned our sins – he canceled the bond that stood against us!" (Colossians 1:12-14) And the gospel of Luke states: "When we pray say, Our Father... forgive us our sins, for we too forgive all who do us wrong!" (Luke 11:1-13) The Biblical message describes a threefold forgiveness. God forgives us. God is very much like the prodigal father who welcomes back his runaway child. We are therefore urged to forgive ourselves. The great commandment tells us to love God, love neighbor precisely the way we love ourselves. We are not supposed to beat ourselves up, hate ourselves because we have failed or sinned or messed up. Jesus, the Good Shepherd, leaves the ninety-nine sheep to find the one lost sheep. It is said that there is more rejoicing in heaven over one repentant sinner than ninety-nine righteous. Jesus forgives us because he loves us and not because we deserve it. If Jesus can forgive us, we should be able to forgive ourselves.

We also are urged to forgive others. We forgive or pardon the offenses done against us because we ourselves have been pardoned. The gospel tells us that our heavenly Father will punish us unless we forgive our brothers and sisters from the heart. And there is no limit to our forgiveness. Peter is told by Jesus to forgive seventy times seven. Jesus hinged God's forgiveness of us on our willingness to forgive others. The lesson taught in the gospels is that Jesus' message from beginning to end is one of forgiveness. "Father, forgive them for they know not what they do!" is one of Jesus' last words as he hung dying on the cross.

C.S. Lewis once wrote that forgiveness, "goes beyond human fairness. It is pardoning those things that can't readily be pardoned at all." Feelings of anger, betrayal and bitterness certainly are understandable when we have been victimized. These negative feelings don't simply disappear and often enough are just below the surface. Forgiveness can be very difficult. It can seem unfair when we have been offended, treated shabbily or unjustly. We may be tempted to revenge. Revenge, however, is something of an illusion. It merely increases bitterness and anger and achieving vengeance hardly ever brings satisfaction. Forgiveness, therefore, is never easy and probably is never totally satisfying. Why should I pardon? Why should I make the first move? I'm the one who has been wronged! Forgiveness is almost unnatural and especially so when the one who hurt me is not even sorry. Why then forgive?

I guess one reason to forgive is to be set free. A reason to pardon is to escape the vicious cycle of anger and bitterness that can ruin our lives. Closed against pardoning another, even though they don't deserve it, even though they really did harm and are guilty, means that we wind up carrying the burden of that unforgiven hurt, and in doing so, we harm ourselves. The word resentment literally means, "to feel again". Resentment holds onto the hurt, keeps the wound raw and relives the pain over and over again. The word forgiveness, at least in its Greek form in the New Testament, means to release, to hurl away, to free oneself. Forgiveness offers a way out and in a sense breaks the hold or control the one who wronged me has over me. An immigrant Jewish Rabbi once made this statement: "Before coming to America I had to forgive Hitler; I did not want to bring him inside me to my new country!" Often enough the first and maybe the only one healed by forgiveness is the one who forgives.

Another effect of forgiveness, at least sometimes, is that it really does have the power to transform the guilty party. Pardon puts blame aside. Not to forgive means that we trap ourselves and fool ourselves into thinking that we can settle the score. In fact, we can never get even. Forgiveness has the power to change the one who has hurt me. Ghandi once said: "If everyone followed 'the eye for an eye' justice, eventually the whole world would go blind!"

> The other reason that we forgive, of course, is that our faith commitment to Jesus requires forgiveness. We seek to imitate the risen Lord who is in life and death a model of forgiveness. Shaping our lives and histories in imitation of Jesus engenders the virtue of forgiveness. Little by little we become forgiving people. Little by little we refuse to be consumed by anger or the desire for retaliation.

On May 13th, 1981, while greeting pilgrims in St. Peter's Square, Pope John Paul II was shot and seriously wounded by Mehmet Ali Ağca, a young Turkish national. The Pope underwent surgery and then was later hospitalized a second time because of infection. Ağca was arrested and imprisoned for life. Subsequently, Italian authorities released him and he was extradited to Turkey and jailed for another crime. He has since been set free. Notwithstanding this violence and senseless harm, Pope John Paul visited Ağca in prison on December 27th, 1983, and forgave him. Pictures of the scene of the two whispering together in a cell became a lesson that Christmas season in forgiveness.

How learn to forgive? It can only be done in the doing. Like all virtues our ability to forgive comes with practice. We do it for Jesus, for ourselves, and even for the one who has hurt us. Over time, through the cultivation of the virtue, we ourselves are transformed and become forgiving persons. A practical suggestion to become a forgiving person: pray for the grace to forgive! Pray for the grace to even want to forgive! And deliberately pray for the one who has offended you! And then, before you know it, hurt and hate slip away and we discover peace. "Father forgive us our trespasses as we forgive those who trespass against us!"

Finito di stampare nel mese di gennaio 2012
presso Mediagraf Spa - Monterotondo (Rm)